Advance praise for *Common Prayer for Children and Families*

"The best gift to little ones is to share what we know of God's love, trustworthiness, and genius. We first hear of those things in the stories of the Bible and the prayers of the church. This little book of prayers will help keep children and families fastened to God in prayer and praise for generations."

—The Rt. Rev. Robert C. Wright,
The Episcopal Diocese of Atlanta

"Easy to use, practical and spiritual, this book will bring those who use it closer to God and each other. The old standards and new prayers will become so familiar to those who read and share them."

—Pattie Ames, Christian Formation Missioner,
The Episcopal Diocese of Southwestern Virginia

"I could say it is the adorable illustrations that I love about this book, and I could say it is the mealtime prayers and praying throughout the days of the week that add meaningful context to daily family life; however, the real depth of this book is that it will encourage prayer and a prayer life with children."

—Trevecca Okholm, adjunct professor of practical theology,
Azusa Pacific University, author of *Kingdom Family:
Re-Envisioning God's Plan for Marriage and Family*

"These prayers use language that is easily accessible for children without sacrificing depth of meaning."

—Sarah Bentley Allred, Director of Children and
Family Ministries, St. John's Episcopal Church,
Wake Forest, North Carolina

"Rooted in the tradition of common prayer, this book is expansive in its creative use of language and illustration, well-organized for the seasons of the church, and applicable to all who seek the daily rhythm of prayer for life."
—The Rev. Michael Sullivan,
President and CEO of Kanuga

"A much-needed, beautifully written compendium that honors children and celebrates the rich prayer traditions of the Episcopal Church. A wonderful way to enrich prayer life at home, in church, or in school chapel."
—Ann Mellow, Associate Director,
National Association of Episcopal Schools

"In its simplicity, it offers the possibility of a rhythm of prayer that will sustain and nurture the spiritual life across the generations."
—Mary Hawes, National Children and
Youth Adviser for the Church of England

"*Common Prayer for Children and Families* offers accessible and theologically sound ways for everyone in the family to worship and wonder together."
—Amanda Wischkaemper, Director of Children's Ministry,
St. David's Episcopal Church, Austin, Texas

COMMON PRAYER
for Children and Families

JENIFER GAMBER &
TIMOTHY J. S. SEAMANS

Foreword by Wendy Claire Barrie
Illustrations by Perry Hodgkins Jones

CHURCH
PUBLISHING
INCORPORATED

Church Publishing
19 East 34th Street
New York, NY 10016
www.churchpublishing.org

Cover art by Perry Hodgkins Jones
Cover design by Jennifer Kopec, 2Pug Design

Library of Congress Cataloging-in-Publication Data

Names: Gamber, Jenifer, author. | Seamans, Timothy
J. S., author. | Jones, Perry Hodgkins, illustrator.
Title: Common prayer for children and families
/ Jenifer Gamber and Timothy J. S. Seamans ;
foreword by Wendy Claire Barrie ; illustrations by
Perry Hodgkins Jones.
Identifiers: LCCN 2019038882 (print) | LCCN
2019038883 (ebook) | ISBN 9781640652644
(paperback) | ISBN 9781640652651 (ebook)
Subjects: LCSH: Children--Prayers and devotions--
Juvenile literature.
Classification: LCC BV265 .G36 2020 (print) | LCC
BV265 (ebook) | DDC
242/.82--dc23
LC record available at https://lccn.loc.gov/2019038882
LC ebook record available at https://lccn.loc.
gov/2019038883

To our children:
Nico
and
Will and Em

CONTENTS

FOREWORD

Don't be too gentle with this lovely book of prayers you hold in your hands. It's meant to be used daily, and even several times a day. Let it become slightly sticky from letting your child choose a mealtime grace even after they've had their first mouthful of something delicious. Pages will be dog-eared—that's okay, too—that will make it easier to turn to certain prayers quickly. Your children may even want to color the charming line drawings: please let them. Use your family

Christmas card as a bookmark for the Advent pages, and the palm cross you brought home from church for the Lent and Holy Week prayers. And if you never got around to a family Christmas card and aren't sure what a palm cross is, then this book is also for you, because there are prayers for every day and the circle of the church year that will be just enough to help you feel the rhythm of God's time.

Homes are as holy as churches, and our prayers help make them so. Perhaps prayer comes easily to you and your family, and you'll be delighted to add some new ones to those you already treasure. Maybe, praying as a family is new and even a bit awkward; this thoughtful, generous collection will help you get started. In these pages you'll find traditional and new prayers with images of God that will be familiar and expansive language to engage our hearts and imaginations. There are psalms and songs, saints and angels, words to comfort and to challenge us, and three different versions of the prayer that Jesus taught us. Wherever we go, God is with us, so there are prayers for sleepovers, school, and camp. Jenifer and Timothy have found or written prayers for every reason and season. There are prayers for a wiggly tooth and for tragedies, for

taking a test and a snow day, for celebrations and disappointment, for those in need or trouble, for friends of other religions, for remembering that in God we are all one.

We may pray with different understandings of how prayer works and even wonder if it does, but prayer is a way of coming close to God. We pray to give our wonder and our thanks, we pray in joy, in sadness, in anger or frustration, we pray to give over to God what we can't hold alone. Praying as a family and teaching our children to pray is a gift that lasts throughout our lives and one that may last generations.

In this book, Jenifer and Timothy, as parents, priests, educators, and writers, have given us a gift that will also last generations, even if it— and I hope it might—means passing on a sticky, dog-eared, colored-in book. I predict that many of these prayers will be known by heart in a short while, and others, less frequently needed, will be the just-right words at the just-right time. May the prayers in this book bring us close to God and to each other, that we might share God's love with everyone we meet. Amen!

Wendy Claire Barrie
Trinity Wall Street

PART 1

The Lord's Prayer and Mealtime Prayers

Jenifer grew up in a family that ate every meal together, unless they were at school or work. Her family waited weekday mornings for everyone to come down to the kitchen before praying and sharing breakfast. They waited until everyone was home from school or work before beginning dinner. Meals were sacred. And before eating they always returned thanks to God. "Returning thanks to God." That phrase could be unique to Jenifer's family, but it makes sense. Once we acknowledge that all that we have, and all that we are, is from God, even when we pray, we are offering God what already belongs to God. How right it is, then, to return thanks to God before meals in gratitude for the fruit of creation and work of human hands.

We encourage you to join a practice of eating meals together as a family frequently. Light a candle. Take your time and linger over the food with conversation about the day or week. Begin a practice of eating together and praying even if your children are infants. Hold their hands or place your hand on their heads as you pray. They will know the prayer in their bodies. Soon enough, they will want to join. By then you, (and likely they too) will have learned a number of mealtime prayers by heart. When they are ready they will begin to mouth the words and lead them.

When Jenifer's children were young, she laminated a set of mealtime prayers, which were collected into a flip book held together with key rings, and her children decorated them. The family took turns choosing the prayers as they gathered at the table. Find a way that works best for you and your family to pray together.

Let us return thanks to God!

The Lord's Prayer

(traditional)

Our Father, who art in heaven,
    hallowed be thy Name,
    thy kingdom come,
    thy will be done,
       on earth as in heaven.
Give us this day our daily bread.
And forgive us our trespasses
    as we forgive those
       who trespass against us.
And lead us not into temptation,
    but deliver us from evil.
For thine is the kingdom,
    and the power, and the glory,
    for ever and ever. Amen.

(contemporary)

Our Father in heaven,
hallowed be your Name,
your kingdom come,
your will be done,
on earth as in heaven.
Give us today our daily bread.
Forgive us our sins
as we forgive those
who sin against us.
Save us from the time of trial,
and deliver us from evil.
For the kingdom, the power,
and the glory are yours,
now and for ever. Amen.

(Iona Community)

God in heaven,
your name is to be honored.
May your new community of hope
be realized on earth
as it is in heaven.
Give us today the essentials of life.
Release us from our wrongdoing
as we also release those
who wrong us.
Do not test us beyond our enduring;
save us from all that is evil.
For you embrace justice, love and peace,
now and to the end of time.

Mealtime Prayers

Thank You for the World So Sweet

Thank you for the world so sweet,
Thank you for the food we eat,
Thank you for the birds that sing,
Thank you, God, for everything!

(Edith Rutter Leatham)

Back of the Bread Is the Flour

Back of the bread is the flour,
And back of the flour is the mill,
And back of the mill is the wind and the rain,
And the Creator's will.

(Anonymous)

Bless, O God, These Gifts

Bless, O God, these gifts to your use
and us to your loving and faithful service;
make us ever mindful of the needs and wants of others,
through your many names we pray. Amen.

Be Present at Our Table

Be present at our table, Lord
Be here and everywhere adored.
from your all-bounteous hand our food
may we receive with gratitude.

(John Cennick, 1740)

Doxology

Praise God from whom all blessings flow;
Praise God, all creatures here below;
Praise God all saints in heaven above
Praise God the Trinity of Love.

(Thomas Ken, adapted)

Johnny Appleseed Prayer

Oh, the Lord is good to me,
And so I thank the Lord
For giving me the things I need
The sun, and the rain, and the apple seed.
The Lord is good to me.

(Anonymous)

Jesus Prepares a Table

God of love and welcome,
as Jesus prepares a table for us,
let us prepare a table for others,
sharing our food, stories, and lives,
as one body, one spirit in Christ. Amen.

Teach Us to Hunger and Thirst for Justice

Life-giving God,
we give you thanks for the food we are about to eat,
for the earth, animals, and people
that made this meal possible.
Teach us to hunger and thirst for justice;
help us to share what we have with others;
and fill us with your power
to make the world a better place. Amen.

PART 2

Praying through the Day

Two of the greatest gifts Timothy's parents gave him and his siblings were a pair of rituals. Each morning, one of his parents would begin the day with a song, a prayer, and a reminder to receive and share Jesus's love. It was a simple ritual, but it gave each day a joyful sense of purpose and beauty. Similarly, just before turning out the lights each evening, they would take a few minutes to pray together, sing a short song, and reflect on where God was that day. No matter what good or bad events had taken place, Timothy would fall asleep with the faith that he, his family, and all the universe, were held in God's loving arms.

Praying is best done where at least two or three people are gathered, but if you are by yourself that is also okay (we're never really alone since the saints and angels join us whenever we pray). The opening and closing of each prayer in this section is responsive: the leader begins reading and everyone responds with what is printed in bold. The Lord's Prayer, which Jesus taught his followers, is always said by everyone. The morning questions and evening reflections are intended for all. If you like, you can divide the different sections of the prayers among the people present. One person may want to lead while another person reads the Scripture passage or the prayers. Timothy's family rings a singing bowl and lights a candle for the opening seconds of holy silence. During midday prayer, sometimes they'll take turns reading lines from the psalm or canticle; at other times they say it together.

Whatever you do, remember that it's in our nature to pray. Learning to pray is a lot like learning an art, sport, or language—the more you practice prayer the better it feels.

Let us pray!

Sunday: Celebration and Recreation

Sunday Morning

Opening

The Lord be with you.
And also with you.
Let us gather in stillness and silence.

Pause for 10 seconds of holy silence.

God, open our lips.
And our mouth shall proclaim your praise.

Glory to the Father, and to the Son, and to the Holy Spirit,
one God and Mother of us all,
as it was in the beginning, is now, and will be for ever. Amen.

[Alleluia!] Christ is risen:
Come, let us worship.

Song

This is the day, this is the day,
that the Lord has made, that the Lord has made.
Let us rejoice, let us rejoice,
and be glad in it, and be glad in it.
This is the day that the Lord has made.
Let us rejoice and be glad in it.
This is the day, this is the day, that the Lord has made.[1]

Scripture

On the same day he had risen, Jesus was at the table with
his friends. He took bread, blessed and broke it, and gave
it to them. Then their eyes were opened, and they recognized
him. —Luke 24:30–31, adapted

Invitation

Open your eyes to God's mystery. Where will you see Jesus today?

Prayers

God of love, gather all people as one human family.
Guide our community, our country, and the world.
Help us to be kind to all people, creatures, and the earth.
Be with all people who are sad, in need, or any trouble.
May all who have died rest in peace.

For what else shall we pray?

The Lord's Prayer   *Pray together*

Collect

Almighty God, through your Son Jesus Christ,
you overcame death with love,
and opened for us the gate of everlasting life;
lead us into the mystery of the resurrection,
and fill us with your life-giving Spirit
so we can join you in building your kingdom of justice and love;
through your many names we pray. **Amen.**

Closing

[Alleluia] Christ is risen.
Thanks be to God.

Sunday Midday

Opening

O God, make speed to save us.
O Lord, be swift to help us.

**Glory to the Holy One: God beyond us, God with us, and
God within us,
as it was in the beginning, is now, and will be for ever. Amen.**

Psalm 30

I will praise you, O God,
    because you have lifted me up.
Sing to God, you servants of the Holy One,
    give thanks for remembering God's holiness.
Weeping may last through the night
    but joy comes in the morning.
You have taken my sadness and turned it into dancing,
    and you have clothed me with joy.
Therefore my heart sings to you;
    O God, my God, I will give you thanks for everything.
    —*The Saint Helena Psalter*, adapted

Scripture

Sing to the Lord, who has done glorious things; proclaim this
throughout all the earth. —Isaiah 12:5

A Creed   *Pray together*

> I believe in God above,
> I believe in Jesus's love.
> I believe God's Spirit too,
> comes to tell me what to do.
> I believe that I can be
> kind and good,
> dear Lord, like Thee.

The Lord's Prayer   *Pray together*

Collect

> Thank you, God, for the joys of this day.
> **We give you thanks with dancing.**

Closing

> Let us bless our God.
> **To God be thanks forever.**

Sunday Evening

Opening

> God Almighty grant us a peaceful night;
> **and a perfect end.**

> *Pause for 10 seconds of holy silence.*

> The angels of God guard us through the night,
> **and lead us to heavenly peace.**
> Light and peace, in Jesus Christ our Savior.
> **Thanks be to God.**

Confession   *Pray together*

> Loving God, we are sorry
> for the hurtful things we have thought, said, or done,
> and for not doing the things we should have done.
> We ask for your forgiveness.
> Set us on your way and make us whole. Amen.

Song

> Before the ending of the day,
> Creator of the world, we pray
> That you, with steadfast love, would keep
> Your watch around us while we sleep.[2]

Scripture

> So then, if anyone is in Christ, that person is part of the
> new creation. The old things have gone away, and look,
> new things have arrived! —2 Corinthians 5:17

Reflecting on the Day

Where did you see Jesus today? In family, friends, and neighbors? Pets or nature?

The Lord's Prayer   *Pray together*

Song of Simeon

Lord, you now have set your servant free
    to go in peace as you have promised;
For these eyes of mine have seen the Savior,
    whom you have prepared for all the world to see:
A Light to enlighten the nations,
    and the glory of your people Israel.

**Glory to the holy and undivided Trinity,
Three in One and One in Three,
as it was in the beginning, is now, and will be for ever. Amen.**

**Guide us waking, O Lord, and guard us sleeping;
that awake we may watch with Christ,
and asleep we may rest in peace.**

Monday: Love and Faith

Monday Morning

Opening

The Lord be with you.
And also with you.
Let us gather in stillness in silence.

Pause for 10 seconds of holy silence.

Lord, open our lips.
And our mouth shall proclaim your praise.

**Glory to the Father, and to the Son, and to the Holy Spirit,
one God and Mother of us all,
as it was in the beginning, is now, and will be for ever. Amen.**

God is love, and love gives us faith.
O come let us worship.

Song

Rise and shine and give God the glory, glory
Rise and shine and give God the glory, glory
Rise and shine and give God the glory, glory
Children of the Lord.
(traditional)

Scripture

Jesus replied, "You must love the Lord your God with all your heart, with all your soul, and with all your mind. This is the first and greatest commandment. And the second is like it: You must love your neighbor as you love yourself." —Matthew 22:37–39, adapted

Invitation

Who is your neighbor? How can you share Jesus's love today?

Prayers

God of love, gather all people as one human family.
Guide our community, our country, and the world.
Help us to be kind to all people, creatures, and the earth.
Be with all people who are sad, in need, or any trouble.
May all who have died rest in peace.

For what else shall we pray?

The Lord's Prayer   *Pray together*

Collect

Eternal God, who created all things out of love,
we thank you for the gifts of life and faith;
open our hearts to receive your love
so that we might become like Jesus,
loving ourselves and our neighbors just as you love us;
through your many names we pray. Amen.

Closing

God is love, and love gives us faith.
Thanks be to God.

Monday Midday

Opening

O God, make speed to save us.
O Lord, be swift to help us.

Glory to the Holy One: God beyond us, God with us, and
**   God within us,**
as it was in the beginning, is now, and will be for ever. Amen.

Canticle of Divine Love

Love is patient; love is kind.
    Love isn't jealous, it doesn't brag,
Love isn't arrogant, it isn't rude.
    Love isn't selfish, it isn't bad-tempered.
Love isn't pleased with injustice, but is happy with the truth.
    Love braves all things. Love never fails.
Now faith, hope, and love last forever:
    And the greatest of these is love.
—1 Corinthians 13:4–8, 13, adapted

Scripture

God is love, and those who remain in love remain in God
and God remains in them. —1 John 4:16

A Creed   *Pray together*

> I believe in God above,
> I believe in Jesus's love.
> I believe God's Spirit too,
> comes to tell me what to do.
> I believe that I can be
> kind and good,
> dear Lord, like Thee.

The Lord's Prayer   *Pray together*

Collect

> Thank you, God, for faith, hope, and love.
> **We give you thanks with our hearts.**

> Let us bless our God.
> **To God be thanks forever.**

Monday Evening

Opening

God Almighty grant us a peaceful night;
and a perfect end.

Pause for 10 seconds of holy silence.

The angels of God guard us through the night,
and lead us to heavenly peace.
Light and peace, in Jesus Christ our Savior.
Thanks be to God.

Confession   *Pray together*

Loving God, we are sorry
for the hurtful things we have thought, said, or done,
and for not doing the things we should have done.
We ask for your forgiveness.
Set us on your way and make us whole. Amen.

Song

Before the ending of the day,
Creator of the world, we pray
That you, with steadfast love, would keep
Your watch around us while we sleep.

Scripture

When Naomi turned to go back to her hometown, her
daughter-in-law Ruth said to her, "Wherever you go, I will
go; and wherever you stay, I will stay. Your people will be my
people, and your God will be my God." —Ruth 1:16, adapted

Reflecting on the Day

Who was your neighbor today?
How did you show Jesus's love?
Remember that God loves you.

The Lord's Prayer   *Pray together*

Song of Simeon

Lord, you now have set your servant free
    to go in peace as you have promised;
For these eyes of mine have seen the Savior,
    whom you have prepared for all the world to see:
A Light to enlighten the nations,
    and the glory of your people Israel.

Glory to the holy and undivided Trinity,
Three in One and One in Three,
as it was in the beginning, is now, and will be for ever. Amen.

Guide us waking, O Lord, and guard us sleeping;
that awake we may watch with Christ,
and asleep we may rest in peace.

Tuesday: Righteousness and Justice

Tuesday Morning

Opening

> The Lord be with you.
> **And also with you.**
> Let us gather in stillness and silence.
>
> *Pause for 10 seconds of holy silence.*
>
> Lord, open our lips.
> And our mouth shall proclaim your praise.
>
> **Glory to the Father, and to the Son, and to the Holy Spirit,**
> **one God and Mother of us all,**
> **as it was in the beginning, is now, and will be for ever. Amen.**
>
> Justice will make a path for our steps.
> **O come let us worship.**

Song

> I woke up this morning with my mind stayed on Jesus
> I woke up this morning with my mind stayed on Jesus
> I woke up this morning with my mind stayed on Jesus
> Hallelu, hallelu. Hallelujah.
>
> (traditional)

Scripture

Jesus said, "I was hungry and you gave me food to eat. I was thirsty and you gave me a drink. I was a stranger and you welcomed me. I was naked and you gave me clothes to wear. I was sick and you took care of me. I was in prison and you visited me." —Matthew 25:35–36

Invitation

Who do you see being left out or treated badly? How can you be their friend like Jesus?

Prayers

God of love, gather all people as one human family.
Guide our community, our country, and the world.
Help us to be kind to all people, creatures, and the earth.
Be with all people who are sad, in need, or any trouble.
May all who have died rest in peace.

For what else shall we pray?

The Lord's Prayer   *Pray together*

Collect

Compassionate God, who is a friend to every person,
we thank you for the chance to do what is right;
help us to see that others are hurt and in pain
so that we can bring your justice and love to their lives
and show that you are always with them;
through your many names we pray. Amen.

Closing

Justice will make a path for our steps.
Thanks be to God.

Tuesday Midday

Opening

O God, make speed to save us.
O Lord, be swift to help us.

**Glory to the Holy One: God beyond us, God with us, and
     God within us,**
as it was in the beginning, is now, and will be for ever. Amen.

From Psalm 146

Praise the Lord, O my soul!
     I will praise the Lord as long as I live;
I will sing praises to my God.
     Who made heaven and earth, the seas and all that is in them.
Happiness comes to those who do justice,
     And give food to the hungry.
God sets the prisoners free,
     and opens the eyes of the blind;
The Lord lifts up those who show respect;
     God loves the righteous and those who show justice.
The Lord cares for strangers, and gives life to widows and
     orphans,
     but the wicked are led to destruction.
And God will be with us forever,
throughout all generations. Praise the Lord!
—*The Saint Helena Psalter,* adapted

Scripture

Let justice roll down like waters, and righteousness like an ever-flowing stream. —Amos 5:24

A Creed   *Pray together*

I believe in God above,
I believe in Jesus's love.
I believe God's Spirit too,
comes to tell me what to do.
I believe that I can be
kind and good,
dear Lord, like Thee.

The Lord's Prayer   *Pray together*

Collect

Thank you, God, for showing us how to care for others.
We give you thanks with our hands in praise.

Closing

Let us bless our God.
To God be thanks forever.

Tuesday Evening Prayer

Opening

God Almighty grant us a peaceful night;
and a perfect end.

Pause for 10 seconds of holy silence.

The angels of God guard us through the night,
and lead us to heavenly peace.
Light and peace, in Jesus Christ our Savior.
Thanks be to God.

Confession   *Pray together*

Loving God, we are sorry
for the hurtful things we have thought, said, or done,
and for not doing the things we should have done.
We ask for your forgiveness.
Set us on your way and make us whole. Amen.

Song

Before the ending of the day,
Creator of the world, we pray
That you, with steadfast love, would keep
Your watch around us while we sleep.

Scripture

When the king asked Queen Esther what she wanted, she answered, "If it please your majesty to grant my humble request, my wish is that I may live and my people may live." —Esther 7:3, adapted

Reflecting on the Day

Queen Esther was a friend to her people. Who were your friends today?

The Lord's Prayer   *Pray together*

Song of Simeon

Lord, you now have set your servant free
    to go in peace as you have promised;
For these eyes of mine have seen the Savior,
    whom you have prepared for all the world to see:
A Light to enlighten the nations,
    and the glory of your people Israel.

Glory to the holy and undivided Trinity,
Three in One and One in Three,
as it was in the beginning, is now, and will be for ever. Amen.

Guide us waking, O Lord, and guard us sleeping;
that awake we may watch with Christ,
and asleep we may rest in peace.

Wednesday: Wisdom and Hope

Wednesday Morning

Opening

The Lord be with you.
And also with you.
Let us gather in stillness and silence.

Pause for 10 seconds of holy silence.

Lord, open our lips.
And our mouth shall proclaim your praise.

**Glory to the Father, and to the Son, and to the Holy Spirit,
one God and Mother of us all,
as it was in the beginning, is now, and will be for ever. Amen.**

You are the light of the world.
O come let us worship.

Song

This little light of mine, I'm going to let it shine.
This little light of mine, I'm going to let it shine.
This little light of mine, I'm going to let it shine.
Let it shine, let it shine, let it shine.

(traditional)

Scripture

People don't light a lamp and put it under a basket. Instead, they put it on top of a lampstand, and it shines on all who are in the house. In the same way, let your light shine before people, so they can see the good things you do and praise your Father who is in heaven. —Matthew 5:15–16, adapted

Invitation

How can you shine your light in the world? What do you know about Jesus that can spread hope?

Prayers

God of love, gather all people as one human family.
Guide our community, our country, and the world.
Help us to be kind to all people, creatures, and the earth.
Be with all people who are sad, in need, or any trouble.
May all who have died rest in peace.

For what else shall we pray?

The Lord's Prayer   *Pray together*

Collect

Glorious God, who spoke light into the world,
we thank you for sending Jesus, your Son,
as a light for all people;
help us to find the light within ourselves and one other
so that we may rise like the sun
and shine love in all places;
through your many names we pray. Amen.

Closing

You are the light of the world.
Thanks be to God.

Wednesday Midday

Opening

O God, make speed to save us.
O Lord, be swift to help us.

**Glory to the Holy One: God beyond us, God with us, and
    God within us,
as it was in the beginning, is now, and will be for ever. Amen.**

Psalm 147:1–7

Alleluia! How good it is to sing praises to you, O God;
    it is our joy to honor you with praise!
You rebuild Jerusalem
    and gather the outcasts of Israel.
You heal the brokenhearted
    and bind up the wounded.
You count the number of the stars
    and call them all by name.
Great are you and mighty in power;
    there is no limit to your wisdom.
You lift up the lowly,
    and bring down the wicked.
We sing to you, Most High, with thanksgiving;
    we make music to you with our instruments.

—*The Saint Helena Psalter*, adapted

Scripture

Anyone who needs wisdom should ask God, whose very nature is to give to everyone without a second thought, without keeping score. Wisdom will certainly be given to those who ask. —James 1:5

A Creed   *Pray together*

I believe in God above,
I believe in Jesus' love.
I believe God's Spirit too,
comes to tell me what to do.
I believe that I can be
kind and good,
dear Lord, like Thee.

The Lord's Prayer   *Pray together*

Collect

Thank you, God, for your power and wisdom.
We give you thanks with our voices.

Closing

Let us bless our God.
To God be thanks forever.

Wednesday Evening Prayer

Opening

God Almighty grant us a peaceful night;
and a perfect end.

Pause for 10 seconds of holy silence.

The angels of God guard us through the night,
and lead us to heavenly peace.
Light and peace, in Jesus Christ our Savior.
Thanks be to God.

Confession   *Pray together*

Loving God, we are sorry
for the hurtful things we have thought, said, or done,
and for not doing the things we should have done.
We ask for your forgiveness.
Set us on your way and make us whole. Amen.

Song

Before the ending of the day,
Creator of the world, we pray
That you, with steadfast love, would keep
Your watch around us while we sleep.

Scripture

Don't abandon wisdom, and she will guard you. Love her, and she will protect you. Get wisdom! Get understanding before anything else. Highly respect her, and she will raise you up. She will honor you if you embrace her. She will place a graceful wreath on your head; she will give you a glorious crown. —Proverbs 4:6–9, adapted

Reflecting on the Day

Where did you sense God shining in your life today? Where did you shine your light?

The Lord's Prayer   *Pray together*

Song of Simeon

Lord, you now have set your servant free
    to go in peace as you have promised;
For these eyes of mine have seen the Savior,
    whom you have prepared for all the world to see:
A Light to enlighten the nations,
    and the glory of your people Israel.

**Glory to the holy and undivided Trinity,
Three in One and One in Three,
as it was in the beginning, is now, and will be for ever. Amen.**

**Guide us waking, O Lord, and guard us sleeping;
that awake we may watch with Christ,
and asleep we may rest in peace.**

Thursday: Healing and Peace

Thursday Morning

Opening

> The Lord be with you.
> **And also with you.**
> Let us gather in stillness and silence.
>
> *Pause for 10 seconds of holy silence.*
>
> Lord, open our lips.
> **And our mouth shall proclaim your praise.**
>
> **Glory to the Father, and to the Son, and to the Holy Spirit,**
> **one God and Mother of us all,**
> **as it was in the beginning, is now, and will be for ever. Amen.**
>
> I will give peace in the land.
> **O come let us worship.**

Song

> Peace before us, peace behind us,
> peace under our feet.
> Peace within us, peace over us,
> let all around us be peace.[3]

Scripture

Forceful winds arose, and waves crashed against the boat
so that the boat was swamped. Jesus got up and gave
orders to the wind, and he said to the lake, "Silence! Be
still!" The wind settled down and there was a great calm.
Overcome with awe, the disciples said to each other,
"Who then is this? Even the wind and the sea obey him!"
—Mark 4: 37, 39, 41, adapted

Invitation

Do you ever feel like there's a storm going on inside you?
Can you ask Jesus for peace?

Prayers

God of love, gather all people as one human family.
Guide our community, our country, and the world.
Help us to be kind to all people, creatures, and the earth.
Be with all people who are sad, in need, or any trouble.
May all who have died rest in peace.

For what else shall we pray?

The Lord's Prayer   *Pray together*

Collect

Almighty God, who calms both wind and water,
we thank you for being with us when we're tossed and
      turned;
help us to trust in your power to bring peace to our day
and give us the courage to be like Jesus
who stood among his friends to calm the sea;
through your many names we pray. Amen.

Closing

I will give peace in the land.
Thanks be to God.

Thursday Midday Prayer

Opening

O God, make speed to save us.
O Lord, be swift to help us.

**Glory to the Holy One: God beyond us, God with us, and
 God within us,
as it was in the beginning, is now, and will be for ever. Amen.**

Canticle of Peace

Come, let us go up to God's mountain,
 so that the Holy One may teach us the ways
and we may walk in God's paths of peace.
 The word of the Lord shall go out from Jerusalem.
God will judge between nations,
 and settle disputes of mighty nations.
Then they will beat their swords into iron for farming
 and will turn their spears into tools for gardening.
Nation will not take up weapons against nations;
 they will no longer learn how to make war.
Come, house of Jacob,
 let us walk by the light of the Holy One.
—Isaiah 2:3–5, adapted

Scripture

Jesus said, "Peace I leave with you. My peace I give you.
I give to you not as the world gives. Don't be troubled or
afraid." —John 14:27

A Creed   *Pray together*

> I believe in God above,
> I believe in Jesus's love.
> I believe God's Spirit too,
> comes to tell me what to do.
> I believe that I can be
> kind and good,
> dear Lord, like Thee.

The Lord's Prayer   *Pray together*

Collect

> Thank you, God, for your paths of peace.
> **We give you thanks with our walking feet.**

Closing

> Let us bless our God.
> **To God be thanks forever.**

Thursday Evening Prayer

Opening

God Almighty grant us a peaceful night;
and a perfect end.

Pause for 10 seconds of holy silence.

The angels of God guard us through the night,
and lead us to heavenly peace.
Light and peace, in Jesus Christ our Savior.
Thanks be to God.

Confession   *Pray together*

Loving God, we are sorry
for the hurtful things we have thought, said, or done,
and for not doing the things we should have done.
We ask for your forgiveness.
Set us on your way and make us whole. Amen.

Song

Before the ending of the day,
Creator of the world, we pray
That you, with steadfast love, would keep
Your watch around us while we sleep.

Scripture

When Martha heard that Jesus was coming, she went to meet him, while Mary remained in the house. Martha said to Jesus, "Lord, if you had been here, my brother wouldn't have died. Even now I know that whatever you ask God, God will give you." —John 11:20–22

Reflecting on the Day

What struggles did you see or face today? Have you asked
Jesus to calm your storms?

The Lord's Prayer *Pray together*

Song of Simeon

Lord, you now have set your servant free
  to go in peace as you have promised;
For these eyes of mine have seen the Savior,
  whom you have prepared for all the world to see:
A Light to enlighten the nations,
  and the glory of your people Israel.

**Glory to the holy and undivided Trinity,
Three in One and One in Three,
as it was in the beginning, is now, and will be for ever. Amen.**

**Guide us waking, O Lord, and guard us sleeping;
that awake we may watch with Christ,
and asleep we may rest in peace.**

Friday: Sacrifice and Forgiveness

Friday Morning Prayer

Opening

The Lord be with you.
And also with you.
Let us gather in stillness and silence.

Pause for 10 seconds of holy silence.

Lord, open our lips.
And our mouth shall proclaim your praise.

**Glory to the Father, and to the Son, and to the Holy Spirit,
one God and Mother of us all,
as it was in the beginning, is now, and will be for ever. Amen.**

Happy are they who trust in the Lord.
O come let us worship.

Song

Will you come and follow me if I but call your name?
Will you go where you don't know and never be the same?
Will you let my love be shown? Will you let my name be
   known,
will you let my life be grown in you and you in me?[4]

Scripture

Jesus said, "I am the good shepherd. The good shepherd lays down his life for the sheep. I am the good shepherd. I know my own sheep and they know me.—John 10:11, 14

Invitation

What needs of others do you see? How can you trust Jesus, the Good Shepherd, and offer what you have?

Prayers

God of love, gather all people as one human family.
Guide our community, our country, and the world.
Help us to be kind to all people, creatures, and the earth.
Be with all people who are sad, in need, or any trouble.
May all who have died rest in peace.

For what else shall we pray?

The Lord's Prayer *Pray together*

Collect

Loving God, who chose
to live and die as one of us;
help us to hear your voice and follow in your path,
giving ourselves to others
so that we may be united in your love,
living as people of your kingdom;
through your many names we pray. **Amen.**

Closing

Happy are they who trust in the Lord.
Thanks be to God.

Friday Midday Prayer

Opening

O God, make speed to save us.
O Lord, be swift to help us.

**Glory to the Holy One: God beyond us, God with us, and
    God within us,
as it was in the beginning, is now, and will be for ever. Amen.**

Canticle of Living Hearts

God calls us from the nations,
and gathers us from around the world.
God sprinkles clean water upon us,
and cleans us from all the wrong we have done.
God gives us a new heart,
and puts a new spirit within us.
And God removes our hearts of stone,
and gives us living hearts that beat with love.
—based on Ezekiel 36:24–26

Scripture

Be kind, compassionate, and forgiving to each other, in the same
way God forgave you in Christ. —Ephesians 4:32

A Creed   *Pray together*

I believe in God above,
I believe in Jesus's love.
I believe God's Spirit too,
comes to tell me what to do.
I believe that I can be
kind and good,
dear Lord, like Thee.

The Lord's Prayer   *Pray together*

Collect

Thank you, God, for your forgiveness.
We give you thanks with our spirits.

Closing

Let us bless our God.
To God be thanks forever.

Friday Evening Prayer

Opening

> God Almighty grant us a peaceful night;
> **and a perfect end.**

> *Pause for 10 seconds of holy silence.*

> The angels of God guard us through the night,
> **and lead us to heavenly peace.**
> Light and peace, in Jesus Christ our Savior.
> **Thanks be to God.**

Confession   *Pray together*

> Loving God, we are sorry
> for the hurtful things we have thought, said, or done,
> and for not doing the things we should have done.
> We ask for your forgiveness.
> Set us on your way and make us whole. Amen.

Song

> Before the ending of the day,
> Creator of the world, we pray
> That you, with steadfast love, would keep
> Your watch around us while we sleep.

Scripture

Above all, show sincere love to each other, because love brings about the forgiveness of many sins. —1 Peter 4:8

Reflecting on the Day

Is there anything you need to ask forgiveness for to begin the weekend fresh? What are ways we can follow Jesus to become more forgiving toward others?

The Lord's Prayer   *Pray together*

Song of Simeon

Lord, you now have set your servant free
    to go in peace as you have promised;
For these eyes of mine have seen the Savior,
    whom you have prepared for all the world to see:
A Light to enlighten the nations,
    and the glory of your people Israel.

**Glory to the holy and undivided Trinity,
Three in One and One in Three,
as it was in the beginning, is now, and will be for ever. Amen.**

**Guide us waking, O Lord, and guard us sleeping;
that awake we may watch with Christ,
and asleep we may rest in peace.**

Saturday: Renewal and Rest

Saturday Morning Prayer

Opening

The Lord be with you.
And also with you.
Let us gather in stillness and silence.

Pause for 10 seconds of holy silence.

Lord, open our lips.
And our mouth shall proclaim your praise.

Glory to the Father, and to the Son, and to the Holy Spirit,
one God and Mother of us all,
as it was in the beginning, is now, and will be for ever. Amen.

Let me abide in your tent forever.
O come let us worship.

Song

God is so good, God is so good
God is so good, God's so good to me.
God cares for me, God cares for me
God cares for me, God's so good to me.[5]

Scripture

Jesus said, "Make your home in me just as I make my home in you." —John 15:4, *MSG*, adapted

Invitation

How can you make your heart a home for Jesus? How can you live in Jesus's heart?

Prayers

God of love, gather all people as one human family.
Guide our community, our country, and the world.
Help us to be kind to all people, creatures, and the earth.
Be with all people who are sad, in need, or any trouble.
May all who have died rest in peace.

For what else shall we pray?

The Lord's Prayer   *Pray together*

Collect

God of my heart,
whose Spirit dwells in all people;
inspire us to find ways to open our homes
as places of rest and play,
so that we may discover the ways
we share a common home in you;
through your many names we pray. Amen.

Closing

Let me abide in your tent forever.
Thanks be to God.

Saturday Midday Prayer

Opening

O God, make speed to save us.
O Lord, be swift to help us.

Glory to the Holy One: God beyond us, God with us, and
   God within us,
as it was in the beginning, is now, and will be for ever. Amen.

Psalm 23

O God, you are my shepherd;
   I have everything I need.
You give me rest in green meadows
   and lead me beside still waters.
You renew my soul
   and guide me along the right paths.
Though I walk through the valley of the shadow of death,
   I shall fear no evil, for you are with me.
You spread a table before me
   even when trouble surrounds me.
You have anointed my head with oil,
   and my cup is overflowing.
Surely your goodness and mercy shall follow me,
   and I will dwell in the house of God for ever.
—*The Saint Helena Psalter*, adapted

Scripture

God finished all the work that [God] had done, and saw
that it was very good. And on the seventh day God rested.
God blessed the seventh day and made it holy, because
on that day God rested from all the work of creation.
—Genesis 1:31–2:3, adapted

A Creed   *Pray together*

I believe in God above,
I believe in Jesus's love.
I believe God's Spirit too,
comes to tell me what to do.
I believe that I can be
kind and good,
dear Lord, like Thee.

The Lord's Prayer   *Pray together*

Collect

Thank you, God, for rest.
We give you thanks with our souls.

Closing

Let us bless our God.
To God be thanks forever.

Saturday Evening Prayer

Opening

God Almighty grant us a peaceful night;
and a perfect end.

Pause for 10 seconds of holy silence.

The angels of God guard us through the night,
and lead us to heavenly peace.
Light and peace, in Jesus Christ our Savior.
Thanks be to God.

Confession   *Pray together*

Loving God, we are sorry
for the hurtful things we have thought, said, or done,
and for not doing the things we should have done.
We ask for your forgiveness.
Set us on your way and make us whole. Amen.

Song

Before the ending of the day,
Creator of the world, we pray
That you, with steadfast love, would keep
Your watch around us while we sleep.

Scripture

I will bring my people back to me. I will love them with all my heart; no longer am I angry with them. I will be to the people of Israel like rain in a dry land. They will blossom like flowers; they will be firmly rooted like the trees of Lebanon.
—Hosea 14:4–5, GNT

Reflecting on the Day

How did you rest today? Where did you feel at home? Remember God loves you.

The Lord's Prayer   *Pray together*

Song of Simeon

Lord, you now have set your servant free
    to go in peace as you have promised;
For these eyes of mine have seen the Savior,
    whom you have prepared for all the world to see:
A Light to enlighten the nations,
    and the glory of your people Israel.

Glory to the holy and undivided Trinity,
Three in One and One in Three,
as it was in the beginning, is now, and will be for ever. Amen.

Guide us waking, O Lord, and guard us sleeping;
that awake we may watch with Christ,
and asleep we may rest in peace.

PART 3

Praying through the Year

The liturgical year takes us on a journey of faith to come closer to God. We recall the life, death, and resurrection of Jesus, and it helps us rehearse the seasons of our lives. By taking the opportunity to mark the year with special prayers and activities, your family can practice waiting, celebrating, saying you're sorry, noticing God in your midst, and growing.

The church year—which is different from the secular calendar year—is anchored by two major feasts: the birth of Jesus (Christmas) and the resurrection of Jesus (Easter). We begin with Advent and move through the life of Jesus: from birth, through Jesus's ministry, and into his death and resurrection.

The prayers offered here will help your family mark this journey as you pause to light candles in Advent, put up a Christmas tree, set out a crèche, celebrate the arrival of the magi, and later remember Jesus's final days before dying. Finally we celebrate the mystery of Jesus rising from death during Eastertide. Be creative in how your family celebrates the seasons of the church year. You might set out cloth napkins that match the color of the season. (Jenifer's mother did.) A common pattern is blue for Advent, white for Christmas and Easter, green for Epiphany and the season after Pentecost, red for Pentecost and saints' days, and purple for Lent.

Remembering the church year in your family celebrations knits together church and home; it reminds the entire family that faith is lived seven days a week, 365 days a year, in our everyday lives.

Advent

Lighting the Advent Candles

A tradition in Advent is to create an Advent wreath made with evergreen branches fashioned into a circle with four candles, one for each of the weeks of Advent. The lighting of the candles reminds us of the coming of God's promised light into the darkness of the world. Each week, beginning on Sunday, light another Advent candle and watch the light grow as we get closer to celebrating the birth of Jesus.

First Week of Advent

Light one candle.

The people walking in darkness have seen a great light. On those living in a pitch-dark land, light has dawned. —Isaiah 9:2

> As we light the first candle of the Advent wreath,
> we give thanks for the great light of the world, your Son, Jesus,
> who is our light in the world so that we no longer walk in darkness.
> May our lives be a light to others. Amen.

Second Week of Advent

Light two candles.

A man named John was sent from God. He came as a witness to testify concerning the light, so that through him everyone would believe in the light. —John 1:6–7

> As we light the first two candles of the Advent wreath,
> we welcome the prophets who shine your light in the world,
> especially (*offer names*). Help us to get ready to welcome Jesus,
> once again. Amen.

Third Week of Advent

Light three candles.

Jesus spoke to the people again, saying, "I am the light of the world. Whoever follows me won't walk in darkness but will have the light of life." —John 8:12

As we light the first three candles of the Advent wreath,
we give thanks for your great love in Jesus, your Son.
Open our hearts to receive your love
and show us the way to give that love to others. Amen.

Fourth Week of Advent

Light four candles.

*"My eyes have seen your salvation.
You prepared this salvation in the
presence of all peoples. It's a light
for revelation to the Gentiles and
a glory for your people Israel."
—Luke 2:30–32*

As we light all four candles of the Advent wreath,
we give thanks for your great love in Jesus, your Son.
Help us to make room in our hearts for your love
and live in our bodies, minds, and spirits. Amen.

Christmas

Blessing the Christmas Tree

For centuries, in the northern hemisphere, evergreen trees have been brought into homes during the cold, dark winter in anticipation of spring. Today, many households decorate trees in festive anticipation of the gift of Jesus, born on Christmas day. Consider waiting to light the tree until Christmas eve with this blessing:

The light shines in the darkness, and the darkness doesn't extinguish the light. —John 1:5

Creator God, we gather around this evergreen tree
in thanksgiving for creation and your love.
We wait with joy for the coming of your Son, Jesus.
Bless this tree of light, that it may brighten our night
and remind us that Jesus is a light for all people.
Bless us also, that we may give the gift
of light to others. Amen.

Setting Out the Crèche

Setting out a crèche is a wonderful opportunity to tell the story of the birth of Jesus in stages. Consider setting out the empty manger and animals at the beginning of Advent and setting Mary and Joseph on a journey throughout the house as they make their way to Bethlehem. This prayer is appropriate at the beginning their journey.

Mary and Joseph went from the town of Nazareth in Galilee to the town of Bethlehem in Judea, the same town where King David was born. —based on Luke 2:4–5

God of dreamers and hope,
as we prepare for the coming of Jesus,
we ask for your blessings.
Give us grace to make room
in our hearts to welcome Jesus
as we make our journey
with Mary and Joseph
toward Christmas morning. Amen.

Epiphany

Feast of the Epiphany

The magi entered the house and saw the child with Mary his mother. Falling to their knees, they honored Jesus. Then they opened their treasure chests and presented him with gifts of gold, frankincense, and myrrh. —Matthew 2:11

> God of surprises and gifts,
> you revealed yourself as a newborn baby
> and, with a star, you led the peoples of earth
> to worship Jesus, your only Son:
> lead us to see you face-to-face,
> and help us to discover our gifts and talents
> so that we may offer them up to you and your service.
> Let us be Jesus's light in the world today. Amen.

Feast of the Baptism of Jesus

When everyone was being baptized, Jesus also was baptized. While he was praying, heaven was opened and the Holy Spirit came down on him in bodily form like a dove. And there was a voice from heaven: "You are my Son, whom I dearly love; in you I find happiness."
—Luke 3:21–22

> God of new beginnings,
> in the waters of baptism
> we receive your Holy Spirit
> and become one with Jesus;
> help us to live as children of God,
> filled with your heavenly love,
> so that all the people and creatures of earth
> may live happily as one family. Amen.

Lent

Ash Wednesday

The Lord God formed the human
from the topsoil of the fertile land
and blew life's breath into his nostrils.
The human came to life. —Genesis 2:7

> Almighty God,
> you created us out of the dust of the earth,
> and breathed life into us:
> may the ashes of Ash Wednesday
> be a sign that we are human
> and will someday return to dust;
> and may we always remember
> that even though we will die,
> you have promised us the gift of everlasting life. Amen.

Season of Lent

After he was baptized, Jesus returned from the Jordan River full
of the Holy Spirit, and was led by the Spirit into the wilderness.
There he was tempted for forty days by the devil. —Luke 4:1–2

> God of mercy and forgiveness,
> you made us to love you and your creation,
> and to love our neighbors as ourselves,
> but we fall into sin
> when we choose to do hurtful things;
> guide us through the forty days of Lent,
> to come closer to you
> with prayer, fasting, and giving. Amen.

Holy Week

Palm Sunday

The one who enters in the Lord's name is blessed; we bless all of you from the Lord's house. —*Psalm 118:26*

> Praise God, praise God, praise God we say,
> welcoming Jesus along the way.
> Waving our branches of palms we say,
> hosanna, hosanna along the way.
> Welcome to Jesus, our blessed king.
> Praise God, praise God, praise God we sing. Amen.

Monday of Holy Week

Jesus said, "Put on my yoke, and learn from me. I'm gentle and humble. And you will find rest for yourselves." —*Matthew 11:29*

> Walk with me, Jesus, walk with me.
> The way isn't always easy, you see.
> But your love, it reaches up to the sky,
> and carries me, so that I can try.
> The way isn't always easy, you see.
> Walk with me, Jesus, walk with me. Amen.

Tuesday of Holy Week

Jesus said, "Whoever serves me must follow me. Wherever I am, there my servant will also be." —John 12:26

I will follow you, Jesus, by following love,
and earth will grow closer to heaven above.
When we serve others and do good deeds,
when we show people kindness and care for their needs,
earth will grow closer to heaven above
when we follow you, Jesus, when we follow love. Amen.

Wednesday of Holy Week

Jesus said to the crowd, "The light is with you for a little longer . . . While you have the light, believe in the light, that you may become children of light." —John 12:35–36 RSV, adapted

The light of Christ glows in me and in others,
and in the family of God all are sisters and brothers.
It's a light you must see with your heart to believe.
It's a light you can share, you can give and receive.
In the family of God we are sisters and brothers,
and the light of Christ shines in me and
   in others. Amen.

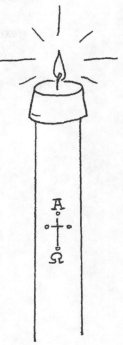

Maundy Thursday

Jesus said to his disciples, "I give you a new commandment: Love each other. Just as I have loved you, so you also must love each other. This is how everyone will know that you are my disciples, when you love each other." —John 13:34–35

> A new commandment, you gave at the table,
> to love one another as you made us able.
> When we love one another, all will know it is true
> that we and our friends, indeed, follow you.
> So let us remember the commandment to love
> so the world becomes more like heaven above. Amen.

Good Friday

*Jesus said, "It is completed." Bowing his head, he gave up his life.
—John 19:30*

> When Jesus died that day on the cross
> all creation together sighed, "This is a great loss."
> Time grew empty and the afternoon dark
> as the light of the world had not even a spark.
> The women stood by at a distance in tears
> wondering what would become of their fears.
> Fear not, the angels soon will say.
> Jesus's death has given us the way. Amen.

Holy Saturday

There was a garden in the place where Jesus died and in the garden was a new tomb in which no one had ever been laid. They laid Jesus in the tomb. —John 19:41–42, adapted

We speak few words this day that is hollow,
this day that sighs with one great sorrow.
We sit in the garden next to the tomb
knowing that soon it will be a womb. Amen.

Easter Vigil

Sing, heavens! Rejoice, earth! Break out, mountains, with a song. —Isaiah 49:13

Alleluia! Alleluia! We sing this night,
joining heaven and earth that rejoice with delight.
Jesus, our Lord, is risen today.
God's love and light is here to stay.
Joining heaven and earth that rejoice with delight,
Alleluia! Alleluia! We sing this night. Amen.

Easter

Season of Easter

*The angel said to the women, "Don't be afraid.
I know that you are looking for Jesus who was
crucified. He isn't here, because he's been raised
from the dead, just as he said." —Matthew 28:5–7*

Through Jesus,
God's love claimed victory over death,
and opened for us the gate of new life forever.
Lead us, risen Christ, into the mystery of Easter
and fill us with your Holy Spirit
so we can join you
in building your kingdom of justice and love. Amen.

Feast of the Ascension

*Jesus lifted his hands and blessed his disciples. As he blessed them,
he left them and was taken up to heaven. They worshipped him and
returned to Jerusalem overwhelmed with joy. —Luke 24:50–52*

God of all times and all places,
when you arrived in Christ Jesus
you began to bring heaven down to earth,
and when you departed
you began to draw earth up to heaven:
bless us so that we may continue
to worship you joyfully in the power of the Holy Spirit,
inviting all the people of earth
to become part of your heavenly kingdom. Amen.

Pentecost

The Day of Pentecost

*When Pentecost Day arrived, a fierce wind filled the entire
house and they saw flames of fire alighting on each disciple.
They were all filled with the Holy Spirit and began to speak in
other languages. —Acts 2:1–4, adapted*

Creator of speech and silence,
Holy Spirit of water, fire, and wind,
we give you thanks for all the languages of the earth;
fill our souls and the Church with your holy flame
and bless our tongues to tell the world
of the love that unites us all. Amen.

Other Feast Days

Trinity Sunday

Say hello to each other with a holy kiss. All of God's people say hello to you. The grace of the Lord Jesus Christ, the love of God, and the fellowship of the Holy Spirit be with you all.
— 2 Corinthians 13:12–13

Holy Trinity, dancing mystery,
you are the Light from Light,
and we worship you as one God:
Lover, Beloved, and Love.
Open our eyes to see that we are your children;
open our hearts to the life of Jesus, your Son;
and our mouths to breath of your Spirit. Amen.

The Body of Christ

We were all baptized by one Spirit into one body . . . If one part suffers, all the parts suffer with it; if one part gets the glory, all the parts celebrate with it. —1 Corinthians 12:13, 26

Lord Jesus,
you invite all people to God's table
to share life and stories together.
Thank you for sharing your body as the bread of heaven,
and sharing your blood as the cup of salvation.
By the power of the Holy Spirit,
as the bread we eat and wine we drink
become part of our bodies
we become part of the Body of Christ.
And we give thanks. Amen.

All Saints' Day and All Souls' Day

You are fellow citizens with God's saints, and you belong to God's family. —Ephesians 2:19, adapted

Today we celebrate the lives of the saints,
who inspire, surround, and support us
on our journey through faith.
Help us to join their friendship and fellowship,
learn from their love, follow in their footsteps,
and lead holy lives that shine the light of Jesus.
Let us also remember all who have died:
whose souls are safe in your eternal love. Amen.

PART 4

Praying through the Growing Season

Jenifer's parents required that, as a young child, she take some time each day to be by herself. Their request annoyed her. Jenifer wanted to play with her brother, talk with friends, or watch television. But she would drag her feet to the hammock in the backyard, for her time alone. Lying in the gentle rocking motion, staring up into the canopy of leaves above, she felt her frustration give way to calm as she noticed the warm rays of sun making their way through the leaves. Their warmth opened her heart and she listened to a voice, its goodness and love.

Her parents wanted her to know herself and God. And they believed prayer, or quiet time, was the way to do that. Their sensibility was formed by their upbringing. As a Methodist, her father reserved Sunday, the Sabbath Day, for prayer for the family. No dancing, playing music, cards, or any of that fun stuff. Prayer meant quiet observation and refraining from activity. Her father knew from the Bible about the many times Jesus withdrew from the crowds to be alone and talk with God—after his baptism, after feeding the five thousand, before his arrest.

But prayer isn't just silence or solitary activity. It isn't just polite petitions. It is honest conversation. Miriam sang and danced after crossing the Red Sea. Hannah wept for a son. The psalmists yelled angrily to God. And Abraham dared to negotiate. These are all ways to pray—singing, dancing, weeping, yelling, negotiating. Let us count the ways! These prayers reflect the true and honest conversation of prayer.

In this section, you will find prayers for home, school, and camp—from learning to ride a bicycle and the first day of school, to fear of the dark. Don't hold back. God wants to hear it all.

For Myself

Joy

Be joyful in the Lord, all you lands;
serve the Lord with gladness.
—Psalm 100:1, KJV, adapted

> Rejoice! Rejoice!
> We leap for joy
> And sing a song of gladness
> because the Lord is God
> and God made us.
> We are God's, always.
> Rejoice! Rejoice! Amen.

Visions

I will pour out my spirit upon everyone; your sons and your
daughters will prophesy, your old ones will dream dreams,
and your young ones will see visions. —Joel 2:28, adapted

> God who visited Jacob, Joseph, and Mary in their visions,
> you have promised that our elders shall dream dreams
> and our young ones shall see visions:
> pour your Holy Spirit into our thoughts;
> let them overflow into what we do
> so that your dreams and visions for us may come true. Amen.

Inner Peace

Jesus said to the lake, "Silence! Be still!" The wind settled down and there was a great calm. —Mark 4:39

> God, who quiets storms to a whisper
> and hushes the sea's waves,
> quiet the rumbling noises inside me,
> smooth the sharp edges of my soul,
> and give me peace
> in this stormy time. Amen.

Health

Peter turned to the woman and said, "Tabitha, get up!" She opened her eyes, saw Peter, and sat up. He gave her his hand and raised her up. —Acts 9:40b–41a

> O God, who is my strength,
> just as Peter called Tabitha to rise up,
> fill my heart with faith in your love:
> give me a calm and patient spirit
> so that all that hurts this day
> can be open to your healing power
> and I may rise again. Amen.

Safety

I am with you now, I will protect you everywhere you go, and
I will bring you back to this land. —Genesis 28:15

> God, whose glory fills the whole world,
> and who is with us wherever we go:
> protect us in our daily lives and travels;
> surround us with your loving care;
> guard us from every danger;
> and bring us safely into the day's end. Amen.

Anger

Know this, my dear brothers and sisters:
everyone should be quick to listen, slow
to speak, and slow to grow angry. —James 1:19

> Almighty and loving God,
> you made us in your image,
> and even you get angry sometimes;
> when we find ourselves mad or angry
> help us to stay under control, not to lose our temper,
> and guide us to behave in ways that lead to peace. Amen.

Disappointment

I put all my hope in you, O God. You lean down to me;
you listen to my cry for help. —Psalm 40:1, adapted

> Loving God,
> you are with us in the good times and the bad;
> when life doesn't go as planned,
> when we are disappointed with others,
> with the world, or with ourselves,
> listen to our prayer,
> send your Holy Spirit to comfort us,
> and wrap us in your everlasting arms. Amen.

Patience

Love is patient, love is kind. —1 Corinthians 13:4

> Eternal God,
> when it feels like life is moving too slow,
> or that we're moving too fast,
> give us the patience of Jesus.
> Help us to breathe deeply and focus our attention,
> so that we may live in the moment
> and be present to ourselves, to our world, and to you. Amen.

Self-dedication

God be in my head,
    And in my understanding
God be in my eyes,
    And in my looking
God be in my mouth,
    And in my speaking.
God be in my heart,
    And in my thinking
God be at my end,
    And at my departing.[6]

Forgiveness

Be kind, compassionate, and forgiving to each other, in the same way God forgave you in Christ. —Ephesians 4:32

God of compassion,
we are sorry that we
have not always done what you wanted us to do.
We have not loved you with our whole heart,
and we have not cared enough
for other people and the earth.
Forgive us, for Jesus's sake. Amen.

Loneliness

"I'm convinced that nothing can separate us from God's love in Christ Jesus our Lord." —Romans 8:38

Jesus, our brother and friend,
you know what it's like to be lonely,
to be without friends or family.
When we feel like we are all alone,
separated from the people we love,
help us to remember your promise
that you are with us always,
and there is nothing that can separate us
from the love of God. Amen.

Sadness

Weeping may linger for the night, but joy comes with the morning. —Psalm 30:5, NRSV

Jesus, you were not afraid to hide your sadness:
you were sad and cried with others
when Lazarus had died;
you were sad and cried for others
when you saw your city reject God's love;
you were sad and cried for yourself
when you were overwhelmed;
but you had faith that sadness doesn't last forever:
give us your spirit of hope that, someday,
our sadness will be overcome with joy. Amen.

Courage

I am the Lord your God, who grasps your strong hand, who says to you, Don't fear; I will help you. — Isaiah 41:13

Jesus, you were tempted just as I am.
Guide me in your wisdom.
Teach me what I should do
in everything and at every hour.
You alone know what I need.
You alone know the path.
Show and teach me how to walk it.
Keep me in mind, body, and spirit.
I give myself to you. Amen.

Surrender

Look, we have left everything and followed you. —Mark 10:28

You have given all to me.
To you, Lord, I return it.
Everything is yours; do with it what you will.
Give me only your love and your grace,
that is enough for me. Amen.[7]

Fear of the Dark

The light shines in the darkness, and the darkness doesn't extinguish the light. — John 1:5

God who gave us the morning star,
to bring light to the darkness of the world,
I am afraid of the dark and the shadows of the night.
Make my darkness bright until the morning light
reveals the day once again. Amen.

Life at Home

Family

God, our treasury of blessings,
come live with us at our home.
Bless us and guide us in your ways.
Widen our hearts to welcome others.
Bind our hearts together
so that Christ's presence
is revealed by our love. Amen.

Friends

Jesus, who is friend to all,
you taught us that the Kingdom of God
is like a tiny mustard seed
that grows into a huge plant,
so big and so strong that birds can build nests in it.
May our friendships grow so big and wide
that they include people of many kinds.
May our friendships grow so deep and tall
that they bring us closer to you. Amen.

Birthdays

O God, our times are in your hand:
Look with favor, we pray, on your child *(Name)*
at the beginning of another year.
Grant that *(Name)* may grow in wisdom and grace,
and strengthen *(Name)* to trust in you
now and forever;
through Jesus Christ our Lord. Amen.

Overnight at a Friend's House

You are my shepherd, God,
set me down in dreamy fields,
lead me by peaceful waters,
and give me rest.
Even though I'm away from home.
I am not afraid; you are with me. Amen.

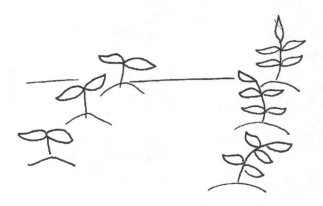

Planting a Garden

Gracious God, source of soil and seeds, sun and showers,
bless and protect this garden and all who keep it.
Strengthen and uphold us as we work in our garden,
that these plants may bear good fruit;
may our care for the earth bear witness to your love and justice;
in the name of the Holy and Undivided Trinity. Amen.[8]

Walking a Pet

As we go for a walk together
may the way that we go be safe, straight, and fair;
may we meet friends along the way, however small or large;
may the sights, smells, and sounds of our walk speak your love.
Bring us home filled with adventure. Amen.

Brushing Teeth

Even in the little things I do today,
teach me, my God and king,
to see you in everything.
Even the little things I do today,
may I do it all for you. Amen.

Bedtime

Holy God, source of all good things,
give me the peace that is yours to give.
Soothe my restlessness as
I give this day, to you, O God,
so I may rest this night
and be ready when morning comes
to share your love with everyone. Amen.

Dreaming

The sun will rise. The sun will set.
I am not done with dreaming yet.
I imagine what my life will be.
It blossoms here inside of me.
So, now, this day, to play I go,
To discover what I already know.[9]

Traveling

May the road rise up to meet you.
May the wind be always at your back.
May the sun shine warm upon your face,
May the rain fall soft upon your fields.
Until we meet again,
May God hold you in the hollow of his hand.
(Traditional Irish)

Going Out for the Day

A parent or caregiver can say this Aaronic blessing over a child leaving for school in the morning.

The Lord bless you and keep you;
the Lord make his face to shine upon you, and be gracious to you;
the Lord lift up his countenance upon you, and give you peace.
—Numbers 6:24–26, NRSV

Wiggly Tooth

Dear God, you know when I sit down and when I stand up.
You know even the number of hairs on my head.
I've got a wiggly tooth.
So you know about this tooth, too.
I'm growing up. I am scared.
Make me brave.
May it wiggle, wiggle, wiggle.
Pop and out! Amen.

Learning to Ride a Bicycle

Spirit God, you are always on the move,
we give thanks for wheels and pedals
that take us to new places
for balance and for pathways
on adventures yet to know.
Protect us from spills and crashes
and keep us close to you. Amen.

Death of a Pet

Dear God, *(name of pet)* died today.
I'm in need of prayer.
Dear God, welcome *him/her* into your arms.
I'm in need of prayer.
Dear God, I miss *(name of pet)*.
I'm in need of prayer. Amen.

Death of a Friend

God of mercy and love that never dies,
receive our friend, *(name of friend)*,
    into your everlasting arms;
welcome *(Name)* into the company
    of your angels and saints
who share in your glorious kingdom of heaven;
grant *(Name)* eternal rest,
and may the soul of *(Name)*, and all the souls of
    the faithful departed, rest in peace. Amen.

Death of a Parent

We give *mom/dad* back to you, God,
who gave *them* to us.
Just as you did not lose *them* by giving *them* to us,
we do not lose *them* in returning *them* to you.
What is yours is ours, always if we are yours.
Life is eternal and love lasts forever.
Death is only what is beyond what we can see. Amen.[10]

Death of a Grandparent

Faithful God, whose love is bigger than the universe,
my *grandma/grandpa* has died and I miss *them*.
Open your arms and hold *them* for me.
Say how much I miss *them*.
Faithful God, whose love is stronger than death,
grandma/grandpa has died and I miss *them*. Amen.

Life at School

First Day of School

Lead me, guide me along the way,
for if you lead me, I cannot stray.
Lord, let me walk each day with thee.
Lead me, O Lord, lead me.[11]

Schools

God of wisdom and truth,
we lift our hearts to you,
giving thanks for the life we share in schools;
we thank you for learning and discovery,
for arts to make and games to play,
and, most of all,
for loving teachers and caring classmates.
Teach us to understand one another,
and grow together in goodness and peace;
through your many names we pray. Amen.

Students

God of infinite growth,
we pray for ourselves and students everywhere;
bring us closer to your love and truth
through our studies, arts, music, and sports;
use us to make the world a better place;
and guide us to deepen our love for you and our neighbors;
through your many names we pray. Amen.

Teachers

God of learning,
we thank you for the teachers at this school
and teachers around the world;
pour out your Spirit upon them
to be good examples of your love, kindness, and wisdom;
give them the joy of seeing their students
laugh, learn, and grow closer together;
through your many names we pray. Amen.

Parents

God of the whole human family,
we lift our parents up to you:
wherever they are,
pour out your Spirit upon all mothers and fathers,
be with them and all caregivers,
and give them wisdom and patience to be like you,
our Heavenly Parent;
through your many names we pray. Amen.

All Who Work at My School

God of gratitude,
we thank you for our friends who keep my school working,
for those who prepare and serve food,
for those who work in offices and libraries,
and for the security that keeps us safe;
help us to say "thank you" with our words,
to be respectful with our actions and attitudes,
and to make this school a great place to work and to learn;
through your many names we pray. Amen.

A New Student

May God bless and protect our new friend _____;
may God show mercy and kindness;
may God give goodness and peace;
and may we always celebrate, love, and respect *(Name)*,
our new classmate and fellow child of God. Amen.

A Friend Who Is Leaving

God of journeys and new beginnings,
you have prepared a new place
for our friend to continue to grow,
to make new friends
and explore new places.
In this season of change,
send your Spirit to give them courage and calm;
may our friendship and love
be with them now and forever. Amen.

Graduating Students

God of journeys and new beginnings,
we praise you for all you have given
and all you still have in store for us;
we thank you for bringing this graduating class
to a new time of growth and possibility;
may you always protect them on life's journey,
and may they always be examples of your loving-kindness. Amen.

The End of a School Year

God of endings and new beginnings,
we are finishing a year of school,
and we are thankful;
we have studied and played,
we have loved and grown,
and we are ready for a long and joy-filled rest.
Bless this school year now ending,
bless our teachers, classmates, and everyone in our community.
May our bodies stay well,
our hearts and minds open,
and may all of our education help to serve this world
that you love so dearly. Amen.[12]

Before Taking a Test

Come, Holy Spirit,
be light to my mind,
and peace to my soul,
that I may work with confidence
and do my best on this test;
to you, who love me
no matter how I perform,
be thanks and praise
now and forever. Amen.

Before a Competition

God of activities and athletics,
grant that we perform with courage, joy,
and respect for any opponents or competition;
may we obey the rules,
so that, win or lose,
we bring honor to your Holy Name
now and forever. Amen.

Before a Performance

God of arts and the imagination,
may we perform with courage and joy;
may our hard work and practice
result in art that inspires the audience
and gives glory to you,
the Artist of all creation. Amen.

Before a Class Trip

God of all times and all places,
be with us as we travel;
help us be respectful of those we meet,
grateful for those who welcome us,
patient and kind to one another,
alert to the wonders of your world,
and confident in new situations;
remind us of your loving presence,
and bring us safely home. Amen.

A Snow Day

God of rain and snow, dew and frost,
you made the seasons with their diverse gifts.
Send us just enough snow this day
that we may receive the blessing of a day at home,
with time to make snow angels and snow forts
and time to play with friends and family.
Keep safe those who plow our streets, clear our sidewalks,
and all those who must make their way to work this day.
Soften the hearts of those who decide to call a snow day. Amen.[13]

Life at Camp

Leaving for Camp

Bless us, O God, as we leave for camp,
set our feet on the path of adventure,
prepare our hearts for new friendships,
show us the way to give you glory, and
through our days at camp,
may our faith in you increase and deepen. Amen.

Blessing of a Cabin

Jesus, who promised to be with us always,
we welcome you into our cabin,
our home for a little while.
Bless this space for friendship, fun, and rest.
Bless us also that we may always remember,
wherever we are, we make our home in you. Amen.

Gathering around a Campfire

God of life and light, we gather before you
around this great fire
as members of your great family,
part of the communion of saints.
Set our hearts and voices on fire with your love
that we may reflect your faithful presence.
Be in our stories and in our songs this night.
Be in our laughter and in our joy.
And when the night draws to a close
and our eyes grow heavy,
be in our rest and renewal. Amen.

Counselors

As we begin our time at camp,
be with our brave counselors.
May the power of God the Creator guide them,
may the wisdom of the Son instruct them,
and may the work of the Spirit energize them.
May we all know the love of God through one another,
in the name of the Father, Son, and Holy Spirit. Amen.

Campers

Bless our campers today.
May this day bring friendship and joy.
Enliven our senses that we may know
the wonders of your creation.
Bring us to a deeper understanding
of your truth and love
as we play, work, and learn together. Amen.

Family Back Home

God who makes all things work together for good,
we thank you for our families at home while we are at camp.
Guide and protect them,
that in their waking and in their sleeping
they may know and love you.
Pour your Spirit upon them,
fill their days with joy.
As our time at camp comes to an end,
draw us together once again,
renewed and refreshed by our time away. Amen.

PART 5

Praying with the Saints

From the earliest days of his Christian life, Timothy felt a deep connection to the saints. The lives of the saints teach us how ordinary people like you and me are capable of showing God's extraordinary love. In church, Timothy would look up at the stained-glass windows and see images of St. Francis, St. Teresa, St. Patrick, and others looking kindly down on him. They felt like extended family—ancestors who are both role models and holy companions on our journey through life. In his heart, Timothy knew that even though the saints had lived long ago, they were somehow, through the Holy Spirit, still present with him there in the church. Not just that, the saints were present whenever Timothy called to them, whether he was at home, school, camp, the playground, the hospital, or traveling . . . anywhere.

When there was conflict and Timothy felt God calling him to be a peacemaker, he would say the prayer of St. Francis. When he wanted to feel the presence of Jesus more deeply, Timothy would say the prayer of St. Teresa or St. Patrick. And after receiving communion each Sunday, Timothy would kneel beside the statue of the Virgin Mary, light a candle, and ask her to pray for him.

Using the words of the saints to pray, making their concerns his concerns, and following their example of godly living, Timothy eventually felt the holiness of the saints begin to influence his own actions and thoughts. The more he made the saints a part of his life, the closer he felt to Jesus. Now, as a parent, when Timothy prays with his daughter he reminds her that she is never alone. Even though we cannot see them, the saints are always surrounding us, praying with us and praying for us.

The Blessed Virgin Mary

Pour your grace into our hearts, O God,
so that we may join Mary, the mother of Jesus,
carrying your love inside of us,
allowing that love to grow,
following you, without fear,
wherever you'll have us go. Amen.

The Song of Mary

My soul sings of your greatness, O God.
My spirit dances in you, my Savior.
I am blessed with the things you have done,
and holy is your Name.
You have shown the strength of your arm
and scattered the selfish.
You have cast down the mighty from their thrones:
and lifted up those who are small.
You have filled the hungry with good things:
and sent the rich away empty.
You have come to the help of your people:
and remembered your promises.
The promise made to our ancestors,
to Abraham, Sarah, and their children forever. Amen.[14]

Guardian Angels

O God of heaven and earth,
we thank you for guardian angels
who watch over us and pray for us,
who give us courage when we are scared,
and remind us that we are never alone
and always loved;
through your many names we pray. Amen.

Unexpected Angels

God of kindness and new faces,
you often visit us through other people,
especially when we're not expecting them;
help us to treat all of our neighbors,
      near and far,
as if they are angels and gifts from God:
welcoming them, forming friendships,
and sharing peace and love. Amen.

Francis of Assisi

1181–1226

> Lord, make me an instrument of your peace:
> where there is hatred, let me sow love;
> where there is injury, pardon;
> where there is doubt, faith;
> where there is despair, hope;
> where there is darkness, light;
> where there is sadness, joy.[15]

Mother Teresa of Calcutta

1910–1997

> O God, who calls us to be a friend to the least,
> enter our hearts as you entered the heart of Mother Teresa.
> Open our eyes to see the beauty of every person.
> Open our minds to discover how we can help.
> Open our hearts to share your love.

Patrick of Ireland

387–461

Christ be with me, Christ be within me,
Christ behind me, Christ before me,
Christ beside me, Christ to win me,
Christ to comfort and restore me.

Christ beneath me, Christ above me,
Christ in quiet, Christ in danger,
Christ in hearts of all that love me,
Christ in face of friend or stranger.[16]

Evelyn Underhill of London

1875–1941

God who is the beginning, middle, and end of all creation,
open our hearts to the witness of Evelyn Underhill,
who as a young child knew the intimacy of your presence.
May we enter more deeply into the world of prayer
and see the wonders of your love in all things.
In the name of Jesus Christ,
who with you and the Holy Spirit lives in us. Amen.

Teresa of Avila

1515–1582

Christ has no body now but ours,
No hands, no feet on earth but ours.
Jesus looks at the world through our loving eyes,
Jesus walks to do good with our marching feet,
Jesus blesses the world with our helping hands,
Ours are the hands, ours are the feet,
ours are the eyes, we are Jesus's body.
Christ has no body now on earth but ours.[17]

Oscar Romero of El Salvador

1917–1980

Righteous God,
you hear the cries of the poor
and know the pain of those who suffer,
give us the courage and compassion of St. Oscar.
May we see the face of Jesus in the face of the poor,
may we stand beside our neighbors when they are threatened,
may we challenge any people who mistreat others. Amen.

Julian of Norwich

1342–1416

O God, you are our Mother
as truly as you are our Father.
We thank you, God our Father,
for your mercy and grace.
We thank you, God our Mother,
for your wisdom and strength.
You, O God, are the goodness in all things.
Teach us to love and have faith
that all shall be well,
and all shall be well,
all manner of things shall be well. Amen.[18]

Pauli Murray of Durham

1910–1985

O God of justice and freedom,
who gave Pauli Murray a song of hope
when her throat was weary;
When we face difficult times
and are scared to stand up
or scared to stand out,
help us to follow her example:
to live hopefully, speak truthfully, and love bravely,
confident that you are always with us. Amen.

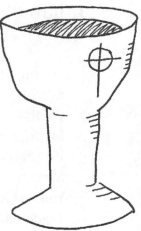

Joanna, Salome, and Mary

God of wisdom and grace,
you created all people in your image.
We give thanks for courageous women like Joanna
who stand with those who suffer.
We give thanks for resourceful women like Salome
who share their abundance with many.
We give thanks for faithful women like Mary,
who spread the news that Jesus has risen.
Give us the gifts of courage, faith, and resources
so that we, too, can be your love in the world. Amen.

Martin Luther King Jr. of Atlanta

1929–1968

Freedom, yes freedom, let it ring
so sang Martin Luther King.
Freedom for you, freedom for me.
For all God's children, liberty.
Give us the courage to stand up tall
to march for freedom, freedom for all.
Freedom, yes freedom, let it ring
so sang Martin Luther King.

PART 6

Praying with the World

"Where is Jesus in the world today?" students often ask Timothy. He tells them how Jesus anticipated this question. In the parable of the sheep and the goats in the Gospel of Matthew (25:31–46), Jesus tells a story where he connects himself to people in the world who are hungry or thirsty, who are strangers or poor, or who are sick or imprisoned. By connecting himself with them, Jesus draws our attention to people in the world who need our help, love, and justice. Jesus is always present with people who are in such need. By caring for them, we are also caring for Jesus.

Baptism also points to where we can find Jesus in today's world. Just before someone is baptized, we promise to "seek and serve Christ in all persons, loving your neighbor as yourself." This means Jesus Christ has connected himself to each and every human in the world through love. Because of this connection, Christians must strive for justice and peace among all people and respect the dignity of every human being.

The point of all of these connections is that Jesus is present with us in our relationships throughout the world. It is the duty of all Christians to pray for and with our neighbors nearby and neighbors around the globe.

The prayers in this section address the needs and the diversity of the world. Almost every prayer is accompanied with a Bible verse that is related to it.

As you pray, open yourself to the presence of Jesus and the love of God in the connection between you and the people you're praying for.

Refugees

An angel from the Lord appeared to Joseph in a dream and
said, "Get up. Take [Jesus] and his mother and escape to Egypt."
—Matthew 2:13

> O God of compassion,
> you welcome all into your kingdom,
> and your love has no borders:
> help us to show love and welcome
> to people from all nations,
> especially those who are running from danger;
> open our hearts so we may open our arms
> and care for our neighbors from other countries
> just as strangers cared for Jesus and his family,
> through your many names we pray. Amen.

People Who Are Imprisoned

I was in prison and you visited me. —Matthew 25:36

> Compassionate God,
> you desire that all people
> be treated with respect and dignity:
> be with all who are held in prison,
> the innocent and the guilty;
> help us make time to visit them;
> give us the vision to see Jesus in them;
> and empower us to show mercy and love
> to all prisoners and their families. Amen.

People Who Are Homeless

I was a stranger and you welcomed me. —Matthew 25:35

God of compassion,
we open our hearts and hands
to all who are homeless,
all who have no place to sleep,
who suffer from the cold,
or who are fleeing homes that are not safe;
we all need a home and a family to love us;
help us to remember that
Jesus lives in the life of the homeless;
guide us to work for your kingdom
where all have proper food and shelter. Amen.

People Who Are Hungry

I was hungry and you gave me food to eat.
I was thirsty and you gave me a drink.
—Matthew 25:35

God who is the source of all things,
you make grass grow for cattle
and plants for people to harvest;
Young lions roar for their prey;
they seek their food from you.
Let us bless God as we prepare food
for those who are hungry.[19]

People Who Live in Poverty

Those who are kind to the poor honor God. —Proverbs 14:31

God of the whole human family,
the poor and the privileged:
we open our hearts and hands to all who live in poverty,
the unemployed and unlucky, the lonely and forgotten,
the sick, the hungry, and the homeless;
fill us with compassion
to see your face in the poor and the powerless;
guide us to work for your kingdom
where everyone has enough
and no one must live in poverty. Amen.

People Who Are Sick

*I was sick and you took care of me.
—Matthew 25:36*

God of mercy and comfort,
you love and care for us, especially when we are sick;
as Jesus took care of those who were ill,
you call us to also care for and comfort the sick;
help us to follow your way of love
and provide health and care to all who are ill,
guide us to prevent sickness from spreading,
and inspire us to learn new ways of healing and medicine.
May we remember when we care for the sick we care for you.
  Amen.

People Suffering with Addiction

Let's draw near to God's throne of favor with confidence so
that we can receive mercy and find grace when we need help.
— Hebrews 4:16, adapted

God of compassion,
we open our hearts and hands
to all who suffer from an addiction:
help us to be honest with them,
and them to be honest with themselves;
give us courage to speak and act in love,
and to help overcome the sources and forces of addiction. Amen.

People Who Suffer from Bullying

Then the Lord said, "I've clearly seen my people oppressed. . . .
I've heard their cry of injustice. . . . I know about their pain.
—Exodus 3:7

Living God,
who sees all the people of the world
as your beloved children:
look especially upon those
who are teased, excluded, and pushed around;
protect them from harm and
keep them safe in your love.
Help the bullies among us to remember
it is never too late to change
from being a bully into a friend. Amen.

People Who Are Hurt and Abused

Carry each other's burdens and so you will fulfill the law of Christ.
—Galatians 6:2

Loving God,
in Jesus you were bullied, beaten, and killed.
You are always on the side of those
whose souls or bodies are mistreated;
help us to embrace those who are hurting;
fill us with your Spirit of healing,
and give us the courage to stand beside them,
and the wisdom to prevent violence and abuse
from happening again. Amen.

People Harmed by Gun Violence

Wisdom is better than weapons of war. —Ecclesiastes 9:18

Loving Lord, Source of all healing,
you weep when love gives way to hatred,
and our souls, once again, weep
for those harmed by gun violence;
where weapons replace prayers,
where peace is overcome with anger,
may our hearts grow bold,
and may our communities be transformed
by our actions and our voices,
working through the power of your Holy Spirit. Amen.

Our Care of Creation

Lord, you have done so many things!
You made them all so wisely! The earth
is full of your creations! —Psalm 104:24

O God, Creator of heaven and earth,
you allowed life to evolve, and you love the natural world:
each plant and animal, each mountain and river,
each ray of sunshine, wave of water, and breath of fresh air.
In our beginning, you commanded us to care for your creation;
open our eyes to see the goodness of the earth;
train our hearts to respect all creation as a gift from you;
and shape our lives to behave in ways that are loving
toward all creatures great and small,
for you, God, made them all. Amen.

People Serving in the Armed Forces

God stops wars all over the world. —Psalm 46:9, GNT, adapted

God of all people and nations,
we give thanks for all people
who honorably serve in the armed services
and devote their lives to making the world a safer place.
We are grateful for their willingness to sacrifice for others;
grant them a sense of your love and compassion,
for those they protect and for their enemies;
guide them to follow their conscience
when faced with hard decisions;
and give us the determination to honor those who serve
by preventing wars from happening in the future. Amen.

Our Jewish Friends

God of blessing, ruler of the universe,
you created the world and all people
and said that it is good, very good.
We give thanks for our Jewish neighbors,
for the ways they show their love of you,
for their care for all people and creation,
for their stories, prayers, food, and celebrations.
Most of all, we give thanks they are our friends,
who join in worshiping you. Amen.

Our Muslim Friends

In the name of the most gracious God,
you have created us in your image,
and shaped us into many people
so that we can come to know one another,
and race toward goodness.
We give thanks for Abraham, our ancestor,
the father of our Muslim brothers and sisters.
Bring us together as one family in your love
so that we may praise your many names. Amen.

Our Hindu Friends

God of eternity and truth,
we give you thanks for the lives
of our Hindu sisters and brothers, near and far;
open our eyes to the beauty of their rituals and teachings,
open our minds to the many forms that Truth can take,
and open our souls to what is immortal;
may the Hindu paths of duty, knowledge, and devotion
inspire holiness within us and throughout all the world. Amen.

Our Buddhist Friends

God of enlightenment and compassion,
we give you thanks for the lives
of our Buddhist sisters and brothers, near and far,
and for the path revealed in the Buddha's loving-kindness;
guide us to dwell in the stillness of the moment,
and lead us beyond our attachments to passing things;
may the noble truths inspire compassion and holy living
within us and throughout all the world. Amen.

Our Indigenous Friends

Many and great, O God, are your works,
maker of earth and sky;
your hands have set the heavens with stars;
your fingers spread the mountains and plains.
Lo, at thy word the waters were formed;
deep seas obey your voice.

Wakantanka taku nitawa
tankaya qaota;
mahpiya kin eyehnake ca,
makakin he duowanca.
Mniowanca sbeya wanke cin,
hena ovakihi.[20]

We Are One Family

God, who called all humans into being,
you long to share your life with all people.
We say "yes" to you in many ways:
Allah, Father, Brahman, Elohim, and Jehovah;
open our eyes and ears when we meet people of other faiths
so we can come closer to you and to one another
as one family. Amen.

TOPIC INDEX

SCRIPTURE INDEX

NOTES

1. Based on Psalm 118:24.

2. Attributed to St. Ambrose. Translated by J. M. Neale, 1852.

3. *Wonder, Love, and Praise,* #791.

4. *Wonder Love, and Praise,* #757

5. *Lift Every Voice and Sing,* #214, adapted.

6. Sarum Primer, Sixteenth Century.

7. Suscipe Prayer of St. Ignatius of Loyola.

8. "A Rite for the Blessing of a Garden," adapted in *The Book of Occasional Services 2018* (New York, The Office of General Convention, 2019), 98.

9. "Dreams" by Marna Franson, used with her permission.

10. Quaker prayer attributed to William Penn, adapted.

11. Doris Akers, *Lift Every Voice and Sing II,* #194, v. 1.

12. Adapted from "Ending the School Year" in *Changes: Prayers and Services Honoring Rites of Passage* (New York: Church Publishing, 2007), 16.

13. Adapted with permission from "A Snow Day Prayer" by Connor Gwin.

14. Based on Luke 1:46–55.

15. A prayer attributed to Saint Francis, partial, The Book of Common Prayer, 833.

16. Attributed to St. Patrick, often set to the tune of *St. Patrick's Breastplate,* an Irish melody.

17. Attributed to St. Teresa, adapted.

18. Attributed to Julian of Norwich, adapted.

19. Based on Psalm 104.

20. "Many and Great," a Dakota Hymn, *The Hymnal 1982,* #385.

ABOUT THE ILLUSTRATIONS

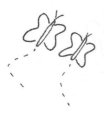

The ink drawings in this prayer book are intended to invite children and families into the scenes through details and characters. The images depict a community of animals who live and worship together in community throughout the year and in and out of an average day. These pictures represent the many ways and reasons we pray and the potential to encounter saints and holiness in each day, even in the ordinary things we do. Prayer can happen anywhere and look like many things. You can pray by yourself or with friends and family. Notice some little details throughout: the solar panels on the church, the rooftop garden and beehive on the school, sunflowers that wake with the sunrise, the little mice who play and pray in the corners, and the name of the church garden (a reference to Leviticus). In addition to the prayers, enjoy getting to know these characters and the roles they play in this vibrant and loving community.

Perry Hodgkins Jones is an illustrator by night and a non-profit fundraiser by day. She grew up in New Jersey and now lives in the mountains of North Carolina with her spouse, child, and two rambunctious cats. Perry is a graduate of Wellesley College and the School of Theology at the University of the South in Sewanee, where she received an M.A. in Religion and the Environment.

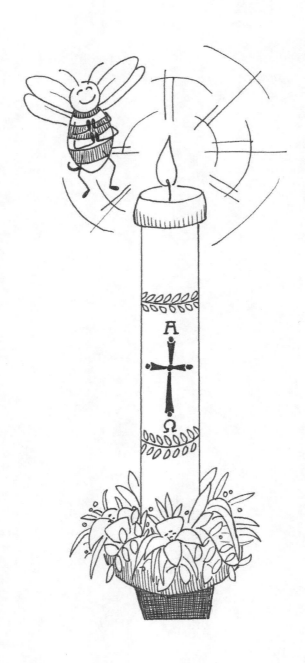